EXPLORERS WANTED!

In the Jungle

Simon Chapman

Simon Chapman
EXPLORERS
WANTED!

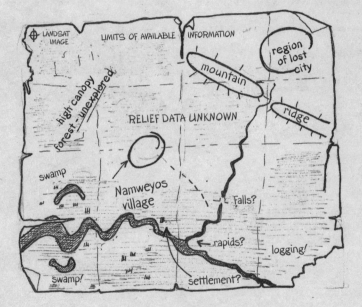

In the Jungle

SCHOLASTIC INC.

New York Toronto London Auckland Sydney
Mexico City New Delhi Hong Kong Buenos Aires

For Joseph – I hope you'll want to come too

ISBN 0-439-86307-4

12 11 10 9 8 7 6 5 4 3 2 1   6 7 8 9 10 11/0

Printed in the U.S.A.   40

First Scholastic printing, April 2006

CONTENTS

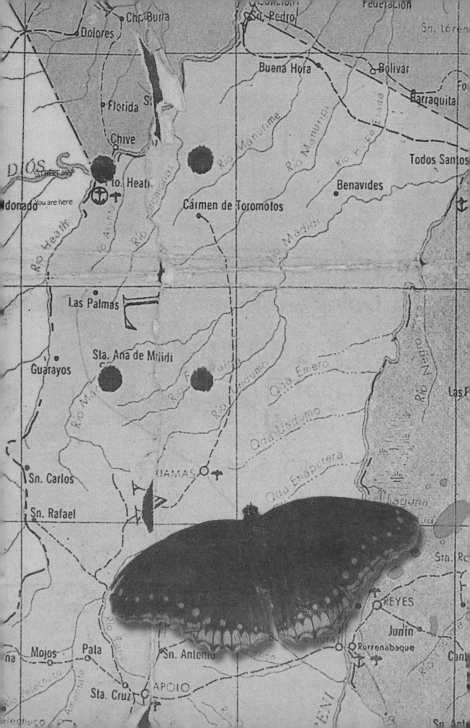

SO... YOU WANT TO BE A JUNGLE EXPLORER?

You want to wander in the deepest, darkest jungles
in the heart of the Amazon rainforest where
NO ONE has ever gone before?

You want to find...

Lost Cities... Unknown Tribes...?

Weird and wonderful creatures...?

If the answer to any of these questions is **YES**,
then this is the book for you. Read on...

THIS BOOK GIVES you the lowdown on life in the Amazon rainforest and essential tips for your expedition, like how to get there, what to take, and **what to expect.** There are also some pretty scary true-life stories of people who have tried to explore it before ... so read on!

YOUR MISSION

...SHOULD YOU CHOOSE TO ACCEPT IT, IS TO MOUNT AN EXPEDITION THROUGH THE RAINFOREST IN SEARCH OF THE RUINS OF A LOST CITY, WHICH IS SAID TO LIE IN THE MOUNTAINOUS HEADWATERS OF THE RIO VENOMOSO, THE "POISONOUS RIVER." THE NAMWEYOS TRIBE OF INDIANS WHO LIVE IN THE REGION HAVE LONG TOLD STORIES OF STONE BUILDINGS DEEP IN THE JUNGLE. THEY CALL THE RUINS "RUCU-RUMIMARCA," WHICH MEANS "OLD CITY OF STONE" IN THE ANCIENT LANGUAGE OF THE QUECHUA PEOPLE OF THE HIGHLANDS. THE NAMWEYOS SAY THE SPIRITS OF THE DEAD HAUNT THE RUINS. CHEWED BONES HAVE BEEN FOUND AMONG THE OVERGROWN STONEWORK, AND A LOW-PITCHED GROWLING HAS OFTEN BEEN HEARD THERE AT NIGHT. BECAUSE OF THIS, THE INDIANS WILL NOT GO NEAR THE PLACE.

IS RUCU-RUMIMARCA ALL
THAT REMAINS OF SOME
LONG-LOST CIVILIZATION?

ARE THERE ARCHAEOLOGICAL
TREASURES TO BE FOUND?

MAYBE THERE'S GOLD!

IT'S UP TO YOU
TO FIND OUT.

YOU WILL HAVE TO JOURNEY THROUGH UNEXPLORED
RAINFOREST TO GET THERE – BY RIVER AND THEN
ON FOOT OVERLAND – CLIMBING UP INTO THE
MISTY RIDGES WHERE THE CITY IS SAID TO BE
LOCATED. THERE YOU WILL HAVE TO MAKE
CONTACT WITH THE SECRETIVE NAMWEYOS, WHOSE
HELP YOU WILL NEED IF YOU ARE TO DISCOVER THE
MYSTERIOUS CITY OF STONE.

Time to set the scene...

Let's find out some vital facts about the rainforest before the mission gets under way.

The Amazon rainforest is HUGE. In fact, it's an area of trees, swamps and rivers the size of Europe. If it's hard to imagine how really vast that is, picture your neighborhood covered in trees, then your town, city or county. THEN imagine that all the way to the furthest place you've been to in a car is forest and rivers, and hardly any roads. Well, that would still only be a tiny part of how big the Amazon is. It is just awesome!

PLANET EARTH

SOUTH AMERICA:
THE AMAZON BASIN

The Amazon rainforest in South America is not the only place where rainforests grow. Here are some other places around the world where tropical jungles can be found.

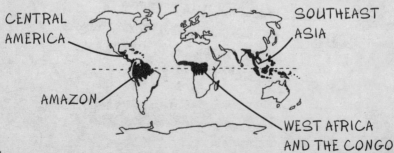

CENTRAL AMERICA

SOUTHEAST ASIA

AMAZON

WEST AFRICA AND THE CONGO

Zooming in on the Amazon...

The Amazon is like a maze of rivers, snaking across the land in sweeping, wide twists. From the air, the rainforest looks like broccoli!

THE AMAZON RIVER

ZOOMING IN STILL CLOSER...

to one muddy river bend on a minor tributary, deep in the jungle...

But what's it like under the cover of the trees?

Everywhere you look, there are leaves and tree trunks. Most of the trunks are thin and tall. Their tops branch out far above your head. This is called the canopy. The leaves here block out most of the sunlight, so everything appears quite dim. Your camera won't work without a flash and direct sunshine only lights up a few small patches.

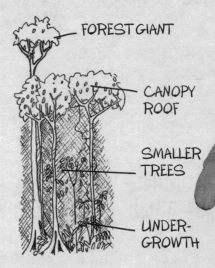

FOREST GIANT

CANOPY ROOF

SMALLER TREES

UNDER-GROWTH

BUTTRESS ROOTS

The ground is covered with undergrowth — small bushes, ferns, and palm trees. Although this is thick in places, it is usually possible to push through without too much difficulty. There are also long, twisted leafy vines that dangle from some of the trees and snake out along the ground.

Occasionally, you come across a tree trunk that is truly enormous; it's propped up from falling over by buttress roots that trail off in all directions.

6

Underneath the canopy, the air is hot and humid. It's not steamy exactly, but feels sticky. You begin to feel very sweaty and damp. Everything smells moldy (and so will you if you stay long enough). Fungus sticks out from dead branches and the tree trunks are blotchy with lichen. Many of the leaves even look moldy and nibbled at, perhaps by caterpillars or maybe by leaf-cutter ants. These ants are probably the first sign of animal life that you notice. They march in long lines across the forest floor, each carrying a piece of leaf, like a tiny green sail, to their nest. Here the ants feed the leaf pieces to a fungus which they eat. There are many other insects around — like blue morpho butterflies the size of your hand. Their wings reflect light when the sun hits them, but when they are closed the back of the wings are camouflaged to look like dead leaves. You'll also be tracked down by mosquitoes which will home in on the carbon dioxide in your breath. They hover around your face and arms, attacking whenever you stand still — sinking their mouth spikes though your shirt and sucking your blood! Unless you are wearing repellent, you will soon have itchy red bumps wherever they've managed to get through — NASTY!

SOUND FX insects, birds	▭ MAX
BRIGHTNESS dim, shady	▭ MAX
SMELLINESS rotten, moldy	▭ MAX
COLOR green, some brown	▭ MAX

Apart from insects, you probably won't see much wildlife at first, but it'll be there, hiding out of sight in the canopy above your head, or maybe in the undergrowth just in front of you.

Suddenly, there is a rustle of leaves ahead of you...

You push forward, past a tree trunk with lots of thorny roots...

You try to keep as quiet as possible and listen out for more movement...

Anything could be behind that next tree...

A jaguar...

Kills by biting through the skull.

A giant anaconda...

Smothers its prey.

A vampire bat...

A real problem when you are asleep. It shaves off a slice of skin from your thumb or big toe and sucks on your blood. You don't feel a thing as vampire bats have anesthetic spit!

SO ... you creep forward through the undergrowth, past some overhanging leaves ...

WHAT DO YOU SEE?

Look carefully at the picture.

You decide to go back to your trail and turn around to look for the way you came ...

| A | B |

BUT...THIS IS WHAT YOU SEE BEHIND YOU.

CAN YOU REMEMBER THE WAY BACK?

First, find the buttress roots where you started on page 6. Remember, they are now behind the other plants you passed on the way. Then retrace your steps to the overhanging leaves.

C   D

THINK CAREFULLY...
IT'S UP TO YOU TO CHOOSE
WHICH DIRECTION IS THE WAY BACK.

A, B, C, or D?

You decide, then turn the page
to see if you are right.

ANSWERS

A. **WRONG.** After ten meters or so, you come across some broken-back twigs that look like they might be your path. You follow the trail as it winds in and out of the trees, until you come to a bare patch of mud where you find a track like this.
It's a tapir print!

15cm

B. **WRONG.** Pushing through the undergrowth, you soon realize that nothing looks familiar. You decide to turn back, but which way is it?

C. **CORRECT.** Like a forest Indian, you have recognized the "landmarks," the leafy vines and the spiky stilt roots that show you how you got into this situation.

OVERHANGING LEAVES

TREE TRUNK WITH
THORNY ROOTS

TREE WITH
BUTTRESS ROOTS

D. **WRONG AGAIN, SUCKER.** All you find is a wasp nest and a type of ant with a particularly nasty bite.

See how easy it is to get lost?

Let's face it, the next step is to get **organized** and **equipped** — find out what to take to the rainforest and how to actually get there!

Isabella Godin
A JUNGLE SURVIVOR

1769: Frenchwoman, Isabella Godin, sets off from Quito (in what is now Ecuador), to cross the Amazon and meet up with her husband, Jean, who left France twenty years earlier. Traveling with her are her two brothers, a nephew, three maids, a slave called Joachim, and three other Frenchmen. They buy a large boat and hire around thirty Indians to paddle it for them.

2 BROTHERS | MADAM GODIN | 3 MAIDS | 3 FRENCHMEN | 30 INDIAN PADDLERS
1 NEPHEW | 1 SLAVE

Several days down river, the party arrives at a village where most of the population have died of smallpox. Petrified, the Indian paddlers flee into the jungle.

The group builds another canoe and finds a villager who has not died of smallpox to steer it for them. Unfortunately, the man is so ill that when the canoe capsizes, he drowns.

13

The three Frenchmen and
Joachim take the canoe
and set off downstream —
they say — to get help.
(Would you believe

Au Revoir! Back soon...promise!

them?) Isabella, her maids and relatives are left behind.
They wait for twenty-five days, but no rescue arrives.

Sick and tired of all the waiting around, they build
a raft out of balsa wood logs, but this falls apart when it
hits a submerged tree trunk in the river. Isabella nearly
drowns, but one of her brothers hauls her out of the water
just in time. The group decides to set out on foot.

Soon they are lost, walking without food through
trackless jungle. Everyone except Isabella dies. She stays
with the bodies for two days, then sets off again, determined that she will survive. For nine days, she lives on what
she can forage – just insects and roots. Her clothes are
ripped to shreds by thorns and vines.

By the time she arrives at a river, her skin is a mass of bites and cuts, and her hair has gone white from all the stress. She must have been a pretty frightening sight to the two Indians who find her and take her to a missionary at their village.

In gratitude, Isabella breaks her gold necklace in half and gives the pieces to her rescuers. But the missionary takes the gold away from them and gives them cloth instead. Isabella is furious. She demands that the missionary give her a canoe and sets off down river where she is soon rescued by a boat that has been hired by her father to find her. A Portuguese ship then takes her all the way down the Amazon and around the coast to where her husband is waiting to take her to France. He canoes out to meet the boat. It's been twenty years since they last set eyes on each other.

But, whatever happened to the other group? The three Frenchmen that had taken the canoe just took off – they never intended to go back for Isabella and the others. As for Joachim, he got to the missionary's village and took some Indians to search for the people left behind. He found the bodies and got back to the missionary's village shortly after Isabella had arrived. He was aboard the boat that picked her up.

Chapter 1
GETTING READY

ISABELLA GODIN WAS lucky. She was determined to stay alive and found help just in time. Many other intrepid explorers who have become lost in the rainforest have not been so fortunate. No one has ever told their stories! So what could you do to make sure this doesn't happen to you? The answer is preparation. You need to find out what you will be up against and work out what to take. You'll have to get "equipped."

When the Waorani Indians of the Ecuadorian Amazon set out to travel across the rainforest, they take just the barest essentials; a blowpipe to hunt birds, some poison for their blow darts, a small pouch containing some food — nothing much more. They move quickly and quietly, hunting and foraging for whatever food and shelter they might need along the way.

WAORANI HUNTER

But is this *really* your style? Let's face it, this isn't very practical for most of us. You will need to keep fairly well covered up against the biting insects and thorny plants. And you will have to carry all the food and equipment that you need to survive.

Outfitting the jungle explorer

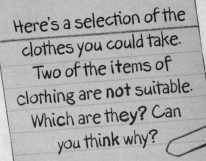

Here's a selection of the clothes you could take. Two of the items of clothing are **not** suitable. Which are they? Can you think why?

HAT

BOOTS

JEANS

TANK TOP

ACE

RAIN PONCHO

SHORTS

SANDALS

FLEECY PULLOVER

LONG-SLEEVE SHIRT

LIGHT PANTS

ANSWERS

In this sort of environment, jeans and tank tops are not suitable. If they get wet, jeans will take a long time to dry. How would you like to walk around the jungle all day in soggy jeans? (This can also be rather unhygienic, as we will see.) As for wearing tank tops, these will leave too much skin uncovered for insects to nibble on.

Now, let's look at the equipment you could take.

The smaller items; a compass, a penknife and fish hooks and line are no problem to carry as they'll fit into your pocket. Really essential items you will need are; a backpack, a sleeping bag, a hammock, a camera, flashlight and batteries, and binoculars.

But what about the other pieces of equipment you'll need? If you could take just seven of the items below, which would you choose?

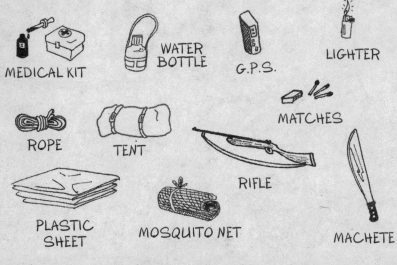

MEDICAL KIT

WATER BOTTLE

G.P.S.

LIGHTER

ROPE

TENT

MATCHES

RIFLE

PLASTIC SHEET

MOSQUITO NET

MACHETE

Work out your survival score on the table over the page...

But first... ever considered taking an accordion to the rainforest?

The English explorer, Colonel Fawcett, was exploring up the River Heath in Bolivia, mapping the border with Brazil, when Guarayos Indians, whose territory they had wandered into, attacked his group. Fawcett and his party — except for an assistant, Gunner Todd — scrambled for cover as the riverbank they had landed on was showered with arrows. But Todd kept his cool. He sat down on a fallen log, picked up his accordian, and started playing and singing "A Bicycle Made For Two" and other popular songs of the day.

Eventually, realizing Fawcett and his men meant no harm, the bemused Indians stopped firing and came out of the bushes to welcome the explorers. They were more used to outsiders shooting back with rifles than serenading them with songs! They took them back to their village and that night, on the river beach where arrows had been flying that morning, they cooked a great fishy feast.

SCORES

ITEM	POINTS	COMMENTS
Machete	60	Essential.
Medical kit	30	Cuts and wounds infect easily in the jungle.
Lighter	30	Warm food will keep your spirits up. Make sure you keep it dry.
Water bottle	20	Away from streams, it can be surprisingly dry.
Mosquito net	20	Mosquitoes carry diseases, like malaria.
Rope	15	You could improvise and use vines instead.
Plastic sheet	15	To make a shelter, but you could improvise using some palm leaves.
Tent	10*	Use the plastic sheet and mosquito net instead. *30 points if you don't already have either of these.
Rifle	5	Not as much use as you might think. What happens when you run out of bullets?
Matches	5	You'll need a fire but these could get wet. The lighter is a much better option.
GPS (global positioning system)	0	No point knowing your position unless you have a map.

150 points and above

Excellent: You've got the makings of a jungle explorer. You are beginning to realize that all you need are a few basic items to survive. Anything else you can somehow do without.

100 – 150 points

Satisfactory: But you need much more training.

Below 100 points

Lousy: At this rate, you'll be starving, wet, bitten all over by insects and disease-ridden before the expedition is over. Get your act together before something large and furry discovers all that tasty human flesh.

Now that your equipment is sorted here's a list of what you're taking.

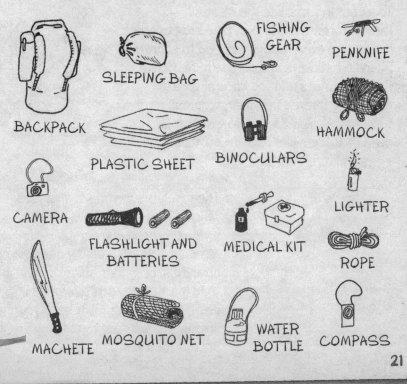

FISHING GEAR

PENKNIFE

SLEEPING BAG

BACKPACK

HAMMOCK

PLASTIC SHEET

BINOCULARS

CAMERA

LIGHTER

FLASHLIGHT AND BATTERIES

MEDICAL KIT

ROPE

MACHETE

MOSQUITO NET

WATER BOTTLE

COMPASS

But hold on, haven't you forgotten about something? What about FOOD? You're not going to get very far without any!

Survival Rations

To forest Indians, like the Waorani, the rainforest is their own free supermarket. It contains everything they need to survive. There are turkeys and pigs to hunt, fish in the rivers, nuts (did you know all Brazil nuts are gathered in primary tropical forest in the Amazon rainforest?), fruit, even delicacies like palm grubs, turtle eggs and tarantula legs!

TASTY PALM GRUBS

HUNTING FOR GRUBS

The trouble is getting all this food, which if it has any sense, will be trying to get away from you. Although you will probably need to hunt, fish, or gather some of your food (particularly protein found in meat, fish, and eggs) to keep you strong, you will have to take much of your food with you.

Take dried foods
like these...

But make sure that you wrap them up well
in plastic bags. Once they become wet,
they will be ruined and inedible.

Don't take vegetables
or much canned food.
They are heavy to
carry and vegetables
rot easily.

For your expedition to the lost city of
Rucu-Rumimarca, you'll be taking food rations
for about 14 days — any more will be too heavy
to carry. Remember, you will have to restock
with provisions that you can find, trade, or
catch along the way!

And don't forget to take...
CHOCOLATE or some other
sweet, yummy food. You can survive
on rice and all the fish that you are
going to catch, but after several
weeks of that...think about it!

Have you collected **all the things** you need? Let's hope so.

Now you should be ready for everything the jungle has to throw at you.

But...

HOLD ON...

Just one thing...

You need some **sort** of transportation.

As the rainforest is so thick and tangled, you'll probably only be able to use vehicles or pack animals to carry your equipment to the starting point of your jungle trip. The point where the road runs out is when the fun *really* starts! Then you'll need something (or somebody) that can carry your belongings through the undergrowth, over or around the hills, and across the swamps. You could hire porters – local people who you pay to carry your stuff – but they need their stuff too (like their own food and camping gear or their whole family!) So, you might end up needing more porters to carry the porters' stuff... and so on and so on!

CIAS - INAR

MIRADOR

Why not do what the locals do and take a boat.

HOW TO MAKE A CANOE

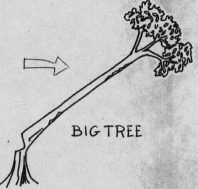

BIG TREE

INSTRUCTIONS

1. Cut down one tree — a big one without any branches sticking out.

2. Place burning charcoal on the log and use an adze — a bit like a pick axe — to scoop out the smoldering wood.

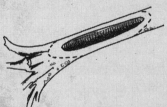

3. Cut and smooth the wood into a canoe shape.

4. To make it faster, add an outboard motor. In Peru, a boat like this is called a "Peke-Peke" after the noise it makes... PEKEPEKEPEKEPEKE.

25

Another way to make a canoe is to peel the bark off a Jatoba tree — all in one piece — and carve it out so that it carve rolls up partly, but not all the way. Add cross pieces to hold it in shape. But you must remember one thing . . . Never take these out!

BARK CANOE
WITH CROSS PIECES

NEVER TAKE THE
CROSS PIECES OUT!

Or you could build a raft. This is FAR quicker than making your own canoe. Balsa wood is good for this (the same stuff that's used for making model airplanes). Balsa trees grow over much of the Amazon. They are a kind of tree weed that springs up wherever forest has been cleared, like around farms and by the edges of roads and rivers. For your raft, you will need dead wood — tree trunks that have been lying around drying out in the sun — as these make the best floats and are easy to find. There is a lot of driftwood lying around the edges of Amazonian rivers.

INGREDIENTS

· Five straight balsa logs — each around five meters long (you'll know they are balsa because they are the only ones you'll be able to pick up).
· Two bamboo poles or straight sticks for cross pieces.
· Rope — if none is handy, you can strip off the inner bark of a living balsa tree.

INSTRUCTIONS

1. Strip off the bark. Pull it up at the end and then peel it away.

2. Cut up the logs so they are all the same length, or arrange them with the longest in the middle and the smallest on the outsides.

3. Tie the cross pieces across, firmly fixing them to each log with rope.

4. Cut a pole to propel your raft, have a practice run and set off.

Paddling upstream

Balsa wood rafts are great if you're going downstream. You can just float with the current. But you'll be going upstream against the flow. That's why you'll need a dugout canoe. This type will be sturdy and solid enough to cope with the rapids and rough water you'll be up against at the headwaters of the river, and big enough to fit in the equipment and food you've decided to take with you.

To start though, the river will be easy — wide like a lake in places with just a gentle current to pull against. And who knows? Before you reach the faster water, you might have found someone who can help you.

Chapter 2
GOING UP RIVER

Expedition Day 1: Food supplies: Maximum

SO, YOU'VE TRAVELED by bus and truck on a very bumpy road to a small village deep in the jungle, where some locals sold you a dugout canoe as well as the food and equipment you'll need for the next couple of weeks. Now you're paddling upstream against the sluggish current... on your own. There'll be no home comforts from now on; no running hot water, no TV, no telephones, no electricity. On either side of your boat is mile upon mile of rainforest. There are no fields, no roads, no houses, no people — no one who can help you out if you get into trouble. Feel up to the challenge? Well, you've made the decision now!

The river you are going up is wide and flat. It's a sludgy brown color. The sun is beating down and you need sun block and a hat to avoid burning (remember to put sun block under your chin as the sunlight reflects off the water). It might be cooler in the shade by the riverbank, but you should try to avoid these areas. Not because of all the caimans, the South American crocodiles you see sunning themselves on the sandy beaches, but because of other things....

SNAGS

Dead wood; fallen branches and trees in the river that have hardened over the years. These could spike right through your canoe's hull.

TURTLES

They stack up on logs sticking out of the water to warm themselves in the sun. They drop off when you get too close.

STINGRAYS

Like a camouflaged dinner plate with a pointed tail. They bury themselves in the sand, so you can't see them. One might whip up its poisoned tail into your leg, as you are pushing your canoe around a snag. The poison won't kill you, but the wound is incredibly painful and might stop you going on or getting back.

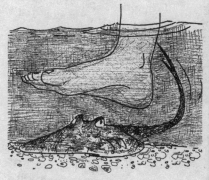

PIUMS

Swarms of midges that leave an itchy blood blister whenever they bite – definitely the best reason for staying in the middle of the river.

Here are some more nasty little biters or "bichus" that might well be worth keeping an eye and an ear open for!

Tabanos

Armored horseflies with a bite like a stapler.

Sututus

These are eggs which are laid on your clothes when you hang them out to dry. They hatch into little maggots that bury themselves under your skin.

Bichus de Pe

Fleas found on dry sand that bury themselves into the hard skin on your feet and under your toenails. Once they die, the fleas split in two releasing lots of little eggs, which hatch out into tiny maggots that itch horribly.

But the worst are . . .

BOT flies

Their maggots get to be 1 cm long. If you ever get a really big boil with a black spot in the middle, smear a bit of grease on it. The black spot is the back end of the maggot's breathing tube (its jaws are busy chomping your flesh). If you cover this hole, it may wiggle itself out a little way, then you can skewer it with a needle and pull it out.

Luckily, all the bichus (except for mosquitoes) disappear by nightfall. The river beaches, with the soft, warm sand, make excellent places for your campsite.

Where would you set up camp?
Think what you would need close at hand.

- Wood for making a fire
- Bamboo to make a frame for a shelter
- Dry ground for a sleeping bag
- Strong trees to sling a hammock
- Clean water
- A source of food
- A flood-free area

Look carefully at the picture
and the possible camping areas.
Will you camp in A, B, C, D, or E?

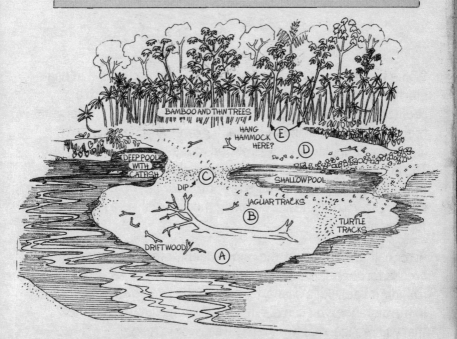

Later, you'll know if you made the right choice.

Some time after you make camp, the ugly, black clouds that had started to well up in the early afternoon finally burst with a boom of thunder, and the rain pours down so hard that it almost feels as if you are being pelted with gravel. Anything that isn't under cover, including any firewood you've collected, is soaked. The high wind that has started loosens old branches from some of the trees. Leaves and twigs fall onto your beach. Behind, in the forest, you can hear a creaking then a crash as a giant tree topples over.

After half an hour or so, the rain suddenly stops and the sun breaks through. It is instantly hot. All the water evaporates, making it feel like a sauna. Further up the river, over the hills in the distance, you can see it's still raining, but it's only then that you realize what this means. The river is rising....

NOW, LET'S SEE IF YOU CAMPED IN A SUITABLE PLACE.

A. **TOO NEAR** to the water's edge. Anything here is washed away as muddy, brown waves slosh down the river from upstream. As it's daytime, you can probably move your things in time, but what if it had happened when you were asleep?

B. **YOUR STUFF IS DRY** at least. Swirling water a meter deep races between you and the shore. The current is strong. Don't try to cross! The water level will go down soon enough . . . you hope!

C. **FLOODED OUT!** Oh dear . . . a total washout.

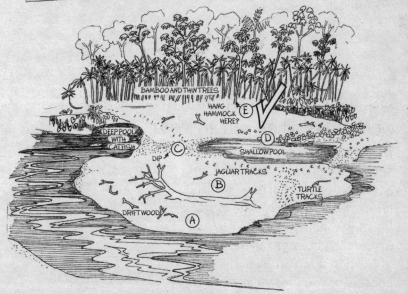

D. A GOOD PLACE. You're high enough up to avoid being flooded out, and there's firewood and good water from the deep pool close at hand. But if you were too close to the forest, you could have been hit by falling branches.

E. A VERY GOOD PLACE. It wouldn't flood, but you should always be wary about hanging a hammock from a tree with undamaged leaves. It might be a "Palo Diablo," a Devil's Pole. They are full of fire ants which swarm over anything that touches the tree, and their sting is like pin pricks of fire. The ants protect the tree and, in return, the tree provides them with special sweet sap to eat.

PALO DIABLO

But what about the jaguar tracks that were there when you arrived?

Well, these are useful if you want to see one. Jaguars often patrol the same routes night after night. This one is probably after turtle eggs. Digging them up to eat is far less effort than going to all the trouble of hunting down an animal like a peccary or you for that matter.

TURTLE EGGS

Here's a thought; you're going to need food too. Where are you going to get it?

You could try and find some turtle eggs to cook before the jaguars get to them, but this would NOT be very ecological. Turtles are becoming rare on rivers because their eggs are being stolen by poachers. What else could you do for food? Well, being by a river, fishing is by far your best option. You'd be surprised how easy this is in the deep pools where the rivers bend. Just tie a hook on your fishing line, put some bait on the end and throw it in.

For bait, a bit of old meat is ideal, but, let's face it, this is not the sort of thing you usually carry around. Of course, once you've caught one fish, you can use a bit of that to catch the next (this works really well with piranhas which don't really mind eating their own kind), but you still need to get started. Think small. Think bugs. Try looking in the thicket of thin tree weeds by the edge of the river.

PIRANHAS

In some Amazonian rivers, these voracious little nibblers are really common. They have a fearsome reputation, but most people in the Amazon are quite happy to swim when piranhas are in the water, except perhaps at the end of the dry season when the rivers are low and the piranhas are hungry.

Take care when taking the hook out of a piranha's mouth. That's when most people get bitten.

Bamboo stems with holes in them are also a good bet; they can contain grubs that you could scrape out with your penknife. Or, you might find insects like crickets and beetles amongst the leaves. If you put one on your hook, it might attract a passing fish. Watch out though for the plant with the unmarked leaves as it's swarming with fire ants.

GRUBS

Of course, if you knew the jungle well like the Amazonian Indians do, or some of the settlers who live along the rivers, you might know some other handy little tricks for catching fish ...

Like shooting at them with arrows. But remember – light bends when it travels from water to air. This is called refraction. A simple rule to help you aim correctly is to shoot the arrow slightly lower than where you see the fish, then aim lower again by one fist's width.

You can also shoot at fish with a gun, but never put the end of a barrel underwater as it could explode backwards. Also remember, if there is a strong current, the fish might float away once you've shot it. Nets and fish traps work well, but they are probably a bit bulky to carry on a jungle expedition.

Some tribes of Indians use certain vines. They pulp them up and throw the mush into a stretch of river that they have dammed up with logs. A chemical escapes from the vine that is poisonous to fish, but not to humans, and prevents them breathing, so they float to the surface where they are easily caught.

THE FLOODED FOREST

In the wet season, many rivers rise ten meters or more. The water stretches for miles into the forest either side of the river, so you can end up canoeing through the treetops. Shoals of fish move into the forest to feed on the nuts and seeds. Predators like piranhas and pink river dolphins follow them.

ARUANA (JUMPING FISH)

UAKARI MONKEY

RIVER DOLPHIN

TAMBAQUI FISH

MATAMATA TURTLE

River people have all sorts of legends about dolphins saving people from drowning or changing into handsome young men at night to dance with local girls. It is very bad luck to kill a dolphin. Many Amazonian fishermen even give them some of their catch.

Thankfully, your night on the beach is peaceful and trouble free…

although you might find some insects that have snuggled down into the warmth of your sleeping bag.

When you get up in the morning, everything is cold, wet and misty. All the water vapor in the air has condensed. Anything you left out on the beach is soaking, and any food you didn't wash up from your plates is covered in ants. You pack up all the wet stuff, cook yourself some breakfast, and set off on your adventure.

The further you travel up the river, the stronger the current becomes. Let's face it, sooner or later, you're going to need help to get all the way up it. You paddle for three days with no sign of people.

On the fourth morning, you see a dugout canoe pulled up on some shingle by the river. On a high bank above, there is a **house**.…

Chapter 3
TRADING WITH MANOLO

Day 4: Food supplies: good; sugar going down too fast — lots of wasps and ants in the package

HOW WILL YOU let the people in the house know you are there? Fire a gun? Shout loudly? Just go up the bank and into the house? And what will you take with you? Your machete — that's a weapon. Is it wise to carry it? You can't see anyone, but chances are someone is watching you. The best thing to do probably is to pull your canoe up on the bank and just wait. They will come to you.

Actually, there's no problem here. A pair of small and very curious children peep out from between some banana trees and pretty soon their dad, Manolo, comes on to the beach to meet you. He's not an Indian, but he looks like he might have some Indian ancestors. He's what they call in Brazil a Caboclo, a river fisherman-farmer.

MANOLO

ROSA MARIA

LEO

ALEJANDRINA

JOSE

He lives in a house he built himself in a clearing that he cut from the jungle. With him are his wife, Alejandrina, and their children, Rosa Maria (7), Jose (2) and baby Leo (9 months). There's also his eldest boy, Marco (9); he's up a nearby river with his uncle who is cutting down trees for a logging company.

Manolo farms, hunts or fishes for all the food his family needs to live. He also cultivates fruits and vegetables in the small garden next to his house.

A. BEANS

B. PEPPERS + CHILI PEPPERS

C. PINEAPPLES

D. SUGAR CANE

E. PAPAYA

F. CASHEW NUTS

G. MAIZE

H. ORANGES

I. COCONUT

J. GRAPEFRUIT

K. MANIOC

L. BANANAS AND PLANTAINS

In addition to that, he has guavas, tea, coffee beans, onions, limes, and various herbs for flavoring food or for medicines. He says that for the moment, he's pretty well set for food, though in a year or two the nutrients in the soil will be all used up and weeds will have started to grow over much of his field. Then he'll have to go to the effort of cutting down another clearing. What he could really do with is a chainsaw, but how would you feel about him cutting down more forest?

TOCO

ALFONSO

RODOLFO

ROSA MARIA

This is Manolo's daughter Rosa Maria with her rainforest pets. Toco the toucan, Alfonso the spider monkey, and Rodolfo the baby peccary. Toco's wings have had the feathers cut across to stop him flying away. Alfonso was orphaned when Manolo shot his mother. Manolo has plans for him — next year's Christmas dinner! This might sound cruel, but this is the only way Manolo can get meat for his family as he has to hunt it or farm it.

Inside the house, Alejandrina is frying manioc flour pancakes for lunch. On the wall are pages cut from magazines. They show Manolo's favorite soccer player, and the Pope.

Manolo says he will help you get the canoe up the rapids in the river, if you're willing to trade some things? But what would he want? He grows just about everything he needs, or hunts it from the forest.

Look at your equipment and decide what you can give him in return for his help.

Think. What will he be able to use that he can't normally get hold of? What can you afford to do without? You have the following:

1. A shirt and a pair of pants
2. Batteries for a flashlight
3. A big catfish you caught yesterday
4. A bottle of aspirin and some tubes of antiseptic cream
5. A machete
6. A sack of rice

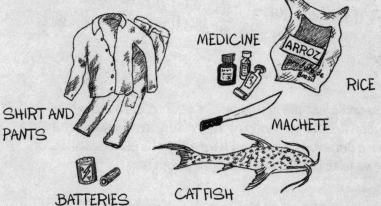

SHIRT AND PANTS

MEDICINE

RICE

MACHETE

BATTERIES

CATFISH

WHICH TWO ARE...

A. Most useful?
B. Fairly useful?
C. Least useful?

Are there any of these things you cannot afford to give away?

MOST USEFUL – Batteries (if you provide several sets) and the medicines – you'll probably have to give both.

FAIRLY USEFUL – Clothes, though he can probably make do with what he's got, and the machete – he's got one already, but he wouldn't say no to a spare. But think! Is a machete a wise thing to give away? Certainly not if it's your only one.

LEAST USEFUL – Rice (depends on how much food he's got – he might be interested), catfish – he can always go out and fish for one himself.

You could just pay him money, of course; even though he doesn't get to go shopping very often, it's always useful. On a more personal level, if you have any pictures, magazines, or news to tell, these would probably work too.

BACK TO THE RIVER JOURNEY...

Two days after you have arrived at Manolo's house, you set off upstream again. The good thing about having Manolo with you is that he knows how to "read the river."

He steers the canoe around the snags and helps pull it up the rapids which have appeared more and more frequently as you start to enter a region of hills.

You can paddle forward by zigzagging from side to side, but if the current is too strong, you have to get out and pull. And don't let the boat turn sideways or else it and you will be swept away. If you fall in, try to float feet first. Head first and you might knock yourself out on a rock. Don't tip the canoe over. If it fills with water, it will be too heavy to hold on to. It might also be a good idea to tie everything in before you set off and put your equipment in waterproof bags, so it doesn't get washed away or soaking wet.

HOW TO WATERPROOF A BAG

You will need:
- One sack
- Latex — sap from a rubber tree.

INSTRUCTIONS

1. Find a rubber tree. If you hear something whistling at you — Weet weeyooo! — the chances are you are in the right area. It's a Screaming Piha, a dumpy little brown bird also known as the seringueiro — the rubber tapper — as it often lives close to rubber trees.

SCREAMING
PIHA

2. Using a sharp knife, score a V-shaped notch on the trunk. Tie a cup or hollowed-out coconut onto the tree trunk to catch the dripping white sap.

3. Leave the cup to fill. Meanwhile "tap" several other trees.

4. When you have enough sap, soak your sack in the liquid and leave it to dry out for several hours.

ARROZ

The Rubber Boom

Until the start of the twentieth century, the world's rubber supply came from trees in the Amazon. Then a sneaky English botanist named Henry Wickham had a gem of an idea.

He took a hundred thousand or so rubber seedlings from the area, put them in little glass-topped boxes (a bit like mini greenhouses), and shipped them to Kew Gardens in London, England. From there, the saplings were taken to Ceylon (Sri Lanka) and Malaya. Most died on the journey, but a few survived and, eventually, these grew up in plantations.

There were two main advantages for planting like this. Firstly, the rubber trees were planted close together, so the rubber tappers didn't need to spend the whole day traipsing around the rainforest. Secondly, outside the Amazon, there weren't any pests that ate the rubber trees, so the plants grew really well.

Nowadays, nearly all the world's natural rubber comes from plantations in Malaysia, but around the turn of the twentieth century — when cars had just been invented and everybody wanted the new inflatable tires — people in the jungle got a bit crazy about the rubber. Various unscrupulous rubber "barons" started enslaving the Indians to tap latex sap for them. They got so rich on the proceeds that cities like Manaus in Brazil became amazingly rich — it boasted an opera house where all the carpets and furnishing were shipped up the Amazon river from Europe at vast expense. They even got Monsieur Eiffel (of the tower fame) to design their local market. But just when everything was going really well (if you were a rubber baron, but not if you were an Indian rubber tapper), plantation rubber came on the scene. Everyone was suddenly very poor and the few Indians who had survived fled back into the forest.

MANAUS
OPERA HOUSE

A RAPID TOO FAR?

Eventually, when going up river, you get to a point when you have to say, "Is it worth canoeing any more. All I'm doing is pulling the canoe through rough water. Wouldn't it be easier just to walk?"

Sometimes, the river makes that decision for you ... when you encounter a waterfall! With little ones, you can unload your canoe and carry it around the side, but there are times when you just have to give in and admit the river has beaten you.

This is as far as Manolo will go. He suggests that you leave the canoe – weigh it down with stones and sink it in a calm pool so no one will find it. Then you will have to walk. There's a Namweyo Indian village maybe three days away on foot to the northwest. With luck, you will find one of their trails that you can follow. He can't say if the Indians are friendly or not, but you made the choice to come on this expedition, so it's a risk you have to take. Don't worry about Manolo. He says he can get back quickly enough. There are plenty of balsa wood logs by the river edges. He'll raft back home. By nightfall, he has gone. ...

AND YOU ARE ALL ALONE!

Chapter 4
ON FOOT THROUGH THE FOREST

Day 7: Food supplies: Original rations down to roughly half. Manolo has left you some bananas and a small fish he caught yesterday.

NIGHT FALLS QUICKLY in the rainforest. There is little twilight, just sunset around 6:30 PM, then darkness. Around dusk and dawn are when most animals are active. The loud noises you hear during the day — birds twittering and insects buzzing — change too. You hear what sounds like trucks starting and telephones ringing. Sometimes you hear grunts and screams, but what makes these strange noises?

NOISE

A. Trundling truck engine

B. High-pitched *poor will p-will*

C. Low *huhuhuhuhuhuhuh*

D. Low-pitched *nunk*

E. *Breep, breep, breep*

CHOOSE FROM...

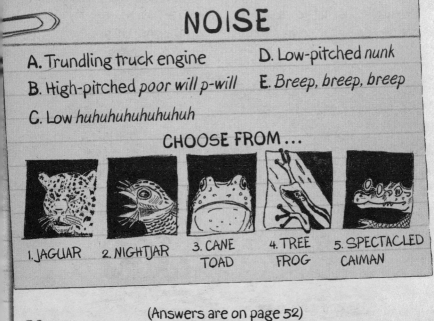

1. JAGUAR
2. NIGHTJAR
3. CANE TOAD
4. TREE FROG
5. SPECTACLED CAIMAN

(Answers are on page 52)

When you shine your flashlight around, you can sometimes see the light reflected back by the eyes of nocturnal animals. For instance, crocodiles' eyes

SPECTACLED CAIMAN

appear to glow orange; spiders have eight eyes, which look like tiny green pinpoints against the darkness. This is because these animals have a reflective layer in the retina (the light-sensitive area at the back of the eye), which gathers as much light as possible, so they are able to see even when there is very little light. "Spotlighting" works particularly well if you hold the flashlight close to your head as the light then reflects straight back. But there's a drawback. The light attracts insects which buzz around your face. Also, some animals have become wise to humans hunting them like this. Big cats, like ocelots, usually look away if you catch their eyes with a flashlight beam. If they stay still, their camouflage can make them nearly invisible.

See if you can find the four creatures camouflaged in the undergrowth.

You found the ocelot, but did you also find the boa constrictor?

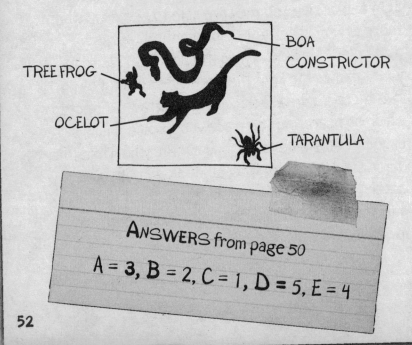

TREE FROG

BOA CONSTRICTOR

OCELOT

TARANTULA

Day 8:

It's cold and misty again this morning. By now you've learnt to keep everything under plastic to stop it getting wet during the night, and wash up anything you don't want to be disturbed by ants or possibly larger animals. As the dawn sun's rays strike the tree opposite, you hear the first shrieks of the macaws flying off to find fruit trees, and a noise that sounds at first like the wind in the trees, a jet engine, then at full volume, like a pride of lions roaring....

HOWLER MONKEYS

"This is our territory. We've got all the best trees. So keep off or we'll do you in."

Howl, Howl Howl . . .

"Oh yeah?"

They do this every morning (and evening for that matter). Each troop bellows out to the jungle.

53

SOMETHING TO TRY ...

Howl back at them. Sometimes they get really annoyed and peer down to look and howl at you. You can do the same sort of thing with lots of kinds of monkeys.

With **spider monkeys**, scream while drumming your finger up and down on your lips. This sounds like a spider monkey food call, the call they make when they have found fruit in a tree; it means something like, "Hey, I've got food. Come and get it." With luck, you'll be able to attract several groups of spider monkeys that will gather around in the treetops to look at you and perhaps wonder why there isn't any food after all.

kiss,
kiss

With **squirrel monkeys**, kiss the palm of your hand very loudly. This is the call they make when they are content and feeding, it means, "Yummy food, hang loose. Things are going well."

You might also try whistling to attract the attention of tapirs (they make whistling calls), but watch yourself. Tapirs don't see that well and you don't want to sound too much like a cute female tapir. A TV cameraman was once chased by a male tapir that had some rather amorous intentions.

54

MONKEYS:
JUST WHAT DO YOU KNOW?
True or False?

1. Only South American (New World) monkeys can grip using their tails.

2. Large ground-living monkeys, like baboons or gorillas, do not live in the South American jungle.

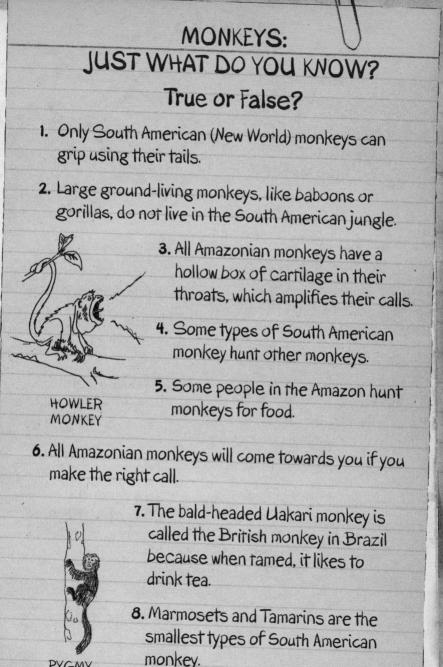

3. All Amazonian monkeys have a hollow box of cartilage in their throats, which amplifies their calls.

4. Some types of South American monkey hunt other monkeys.

5. Some people in the Amazon hunt monkeys for food.

HOWLER MONKEY

6. All Amazonian monkeys will come towards you if you make the right call.

7. The bald-headed Uakari monkey is called the British monkey in Brazil because when tamed, it likes to drink tea.

8. Marmosets and Tamarins are the smallest types of South American monkey.

PYGMY MARMOSET

ANSWERS

1. **True**. South American monkeys such as spider, howler, and woolly monkeys have prehensile (gripping) tails. Capuchins can grip a little with their tails too.

SPIDER
MONKEY

2. **True**. All South American monkeys live in trees nearly all of the time.

3. **False**. Only howler monkeys have this sound amplifier. It echoes the sound in much the same way as the body of a guitar or violin.

4. **False**. Only chimpanzees in the African rainforest have been known to hunt other monkeys. Capuchin monkeys, however, will grab insects, nestling birds, and other live prey to eat.

5. **True**. Large types like spider monkeys are hunted the most. The poor Bearded Saki is also hunted for its bushy tail. Some deluded people think they make great dusters!

BEARDED
SAKI

6. False. Some types
will occasionally approach
you, but not if they know they
are going to be hunted. Brown
Capuchin monkeys called
whistling monkeys (Mono
Silvador in Bolivia) will whistle back
at you if you imitate their call.

CAPUCHIN

WHITE
UAKARI

7. False. They are called the
British monkey because their
bare, pink heads reminded the
local people of sunburnt
English men.

8. True. The smallest is the Pygmy
Marmoset which is about the same
size as a cell phone.

Time to set off on your expedition again

But now you're on foot, you can't carry as much equipment. You'll have to leave some things behind. Choose three items from the list below you can afford to do without. Think carefully now . . .

Machete, bananas, cans of food, rope, plastic sheet, penknife, two one-kilogram bags of rice (you have another two in any case), a paddle, or your camera.

Work out your score from the table below.

Bananas	50 points	Eat them all now, or as you go along, or they'll soon go rotten.
Paddle	50 points	Too bulky to carry, leave it with the canoe.
Cans of food	40 points	Too heavy to carry. As you are likely to return this way, you could wrap up or bury a store of food to pick up later.
Rope	30 points	Again quite heavy. You could always improvise using a vine.
Two rice bags	20 points	Debatable. Wrap them up well and hide them for your return.
Plastic sheet	10 points	You could make do with alternatives like palm leaves for a shelter roof, but plastic doesn't weigh much.
Camera	5 points	Surely you want to take some photographs, but you could leave some of your used films, if you are sure you will be returning by the same route.
Machete	0 points	Survival item.
Penknife	0 points	So little weight and very useful.

Above 110 points

You're getting the hang of this now! You're making the right choices to survive in the jungle.

70 – 99 points

Oh dear! You're going to be wandering around, laden down like a pack mule. Got room for the kitchen sink too?

Below 70 points

Are you trying to make it hard for yourself? Take the canoe and go back to the city where you belong.

When you start out again, you soon find out that it's easier to travel through the shady forest than staying on the river banks where the undergrowth is thick and full of palo diablos and cats claw vines.

Deeper in the forest, it is shady with less undergrowth to cut through. But you still have to watch out for animal holes — you could put your foot in one and twist or break your leg, and take care where you put your hands — watch out for spiky vines or vine snakes. To prevent yourself getting completely lost, you have to mark a clear trail.

HOW TO MARK A TRAIL

- Cut your path with your machete.

- Don't cut your way through thickets. Avoid them. Too much machete hacking scares away wildlife and tires you out.

- To mark your way, cut diagonally through the soft green stalks that slice easily. Mark little notches in the tree trunks; sometimes they ooze blood-red sap which is easy to see (and useful for following on the way back if you get lost).

- Make sure each cut mark is in sight of the one you've just made. That way, if you have to backtrack, you should always be able to see where you are going and where you have been.

- Use a compass to keep to your direction.

- Try to remember landmarks like big trees or unusual looking clusters of vines that stand out in your mind. Then, if you get lost, you will be able to look out for these when you get back on the trail.

towards here

from here

- Make a point of marking trees whenever you change direction.

61

If you decide you are lost, the main thing is... DON'T PANIC!

Stay calm and mark where you are. Remember this point. Go back in the direction you came. If you've been marking your trail correctly, you will be very close to one of your cut marks. And if you find any marks, make sure they are yours — they should be new and still oozing sap. Be careful not to follow trails where you see branches are broken back at waist height (these are often made by tapirs as they go down to the river for their nightly wallow).

You march on through the rainforest for the whole day, marking tree trunks with your machete to show the direction you have come, just in case you have to go back that way.

By nightfall, you have walked for almost eight hours, using your compass to follow the northwest direction that Manolo said you should take to the Namweyos village.

But you have found no village, nor any clearing or path that show that people have ever been there. You have crossed several small streams, where you filled up your water bottles, and skirted around a small swamp, but mostly the forest has been flat and by late afternoon all the vines and tree trunks have started to look the same. You decide to stop and make camp rather than risk going on and losing your way later in the day.

You make a fire to cook your tea and dry out your pants, which are soaked from sloshing through all those streams. You carefully put up your shelter after checking that no branches are likely to drop on you during the night. Then you settle down under your mosquito net and listen to the *breep-breeping* of the tree frogs until, finally, you fall asleep.

Is there anything you should have checked ... considering how nibbled the leaves on the trees close to the campsite look?

Chapter 5

THE RAINFOREST STINKS

Dawn. Somewhere in the Amazon rainforest. Sound FX: Ticking insects, parrots squawking, howler monkeys "warming up."

Day 9: Food supplies. Usable rations low. (You left one of the food bags open and now it's swarming with ants.)

ANTS HAVE ALSO eaten your pants! Leaving them outside to dry was not a good move. They might have been better hung under your mosquito net. The basic outline of them is still there, but now they are more holes than cloth. A trail of leaf-cutter ants snakes off across the forest floor. Some of the ants are carrying fingernail-sized pieces of leaves. Others are holding bits of what definitely look like your pants! There is nothing you can do about them now. At least you have a spare pair, don't you?

Dispirited, you start to relight the remains of your fire and absent-mindedly brush something off your arm. It's another ant. But this one is over three centimetres long! Another leaf-cutter? Maybe it's an army ant.

Or is it the dreaded ANT 24?

Know Your Ant

ANT 24

The twenty-four hour ant (also called a Tucandera), is so named because its bite will lay you out with a fever that lasts a whole day. What's more, this is an ant that also packs a sting in its tail, rather like a wasp.

TWENTY-FOUR
HOUR ANT

LEAF-CUTTER ANTS

They don't actually eat the leaves they collect, but use them to feed fungus that grows in their underground colonies. Leaf-cutter ant "trains" are guarded by soldier ants with specially big jaws for nipping any attackers. Some Indians use these jaws to stitch up wounds.

LEAF-CUTTER
ANT

Hold ant over cut. It bites the wound shut. Twist off the body ... and you're left with ant's head stitches.

FIRE ANTS

They fiercely protect their trees because of the food they get there. They rid the tree of any marauding caterpillars, crickets, and even you if you push against it.

ARMY ANTS

To small creatures, these are probably the most deadly things in the forest. An army of millions of these ants act as a huge team, swarming out in different directions each day from their temporary base with the queen (the only one that can lay eggs) somewhere in the middle. Anything in their path — insects, scorpions, spiders — gets swarmed over and taken back to the nest in pieces.

C'mon boys

Humans and other large animals can usually move out of the way. Ant armies are usually accompanied by "ant" birds, which pick off beetles and other insects as they try to escape.

Ants are found everywhere in the forest. If you were to put all the forest animals together and weigh them — that's all the monkeys, jaguars, insects, and birds — over ninety percent of the weight would be made of just ants and termites! Something to think about next time you're making camp for the night deep in the jungle.

Another thing to worry about.

You smell...
You really reek!

SO DOES THE RAINFOREST. It stinks of fungus and mold. Every leaf and branch that falls to the ground is soon broken down and recycled back into the soil as nutrients. When you step over fallen branches, they often crumble into mush. Termites scurry out.

What's more, all that fungus is trying to recycle you and your clothes back into nutrients too. You reek of sweat and if you don't wash properly, you start getting fungal infections, like athlete's foot in all those sweaty nooks and crannies, under your arms, and between your toes. Your clothes, which are warm from your body heat and damp with your sweat, get spots of black mold and tear easily when you brush past vegetation. And that lets in insects like mosquitoes. Not only do their bites itch incredibly and sometimes get infected, but they can carry dreadful diseases.

In the jungle, you can forget the snakes and the jaguars; these illnesses are far more likely to cause you real harm and some may even kill you! Here's a selection...

Malaria

Caused by a microscopic organism which lives in blood in a mosquito's stomach. The symptoms are easy to spot. You get a very high fever and keep going very, very hot and dry, then cold and sweaty. You feel rotten and your head pounds. Sometimes, you have diarrhea. With one type of malaria, you either get better or die. With another type, you "recover," but have malarial attacks every year or so. Before modern drugs were developed, explorers and local people were always going down with malaria (many still do). The Indians in the Andes used to cure it with a bitter drug called quinine made from the bark of a certain tree.

Note: The cocktail, Gin and Tonic, was created as a way for people in tropical, mosquito-ridden climates to take their daily dose of quinine to ward off malaria. Gin was added to make the bitter-tasting liquid drinkable. Modern tonic water still contains quinine, though as a flavoring rather than a medicine.

Dengue fever/Yellow fever

Dengue fever (muscle and joint pains, a nasty rash), and Yellow fever (headaches, tummy pains, and liver damage that leads to your skin going a yellowish color and death). There's no treatment for either of these diseases except to sit it out (which could take weeks) and drink lots of water.

Leishmaniasis

Then there's Leishmaniasis. This one is particularly nasty. It is transmitted by the bite of a small sand fly. First you get lumps on your wrists and ankles, then gradually your nose is eaten away from the inside. Nowadays, it is treatable, but before modern medicines, you had to use an old Indian cure – grinding up the new shoots of a certain type of tree fern – or eat a well-known poison called arsenic.

Chagas disease

A red and white striped beetle called an assassin bug carries this nasty disease. The beetle lives in cracks in the walls of mud-covered huts. At night, they come out and bite you, after which they poo on the wound– not nice! If you contract the disease, you die suddenly of a heart attack ten or twenty years later, without ever knowing you were infected.

And it's not just mosquitoes that attack you in the rainforest.

 ## Try sweat bees.

These bees just love licking your sweat (which contains salt).
In fact, their tongues on your skin sort of tickles.
They are tiny and don't sting…

So what's the problem?

They come in hundreds. They get in your hair, in your ears, walk right across your eyes, and go up your nose (they love snot). Then, if you squash one, it releases a cheesy smell that is irresistible to its friends. Hundreds more will arrive to see what the fuss is about. What's worse, is that mixed in with these stingless bees there are often other bees — ones that sting! So when you brush them off your skin … BEWARE.

The best way to avoid being licked to death by sweat bees is to keep moving. Remember, mark your way with the machete, and stay quiet. Maybe you might spot some of the wildlife that's been doing its best to keep out of your way for the past few days.

AGGRAVATED ANIMALS

In the rainforest, you won't spot many animals. The forest is too dense and any creature with the least bit of sense will hide itself, or run away rather than find itself face to face with a dangerous and probably hungry human. But there are a few animals who have peculiar ways of acting if they think they are being threatened.…

What might these animals do in that situation?

1. GIANT ANTEATER

2. WHITE-LIPPED PECCARY

3. GIANT ARMADILLO

4. THREE-TOED SLOTH

5. LONG-NOSED ARMADILLO

Which of these...

A. Springs up in the air — then takes off?

B. Looks at you stupidly and slowly waves a claw at you?

C. Rears up on its hind legs and rips at you with its claws?

D. Digs itself a hole?

E. Stands its ground, waits for fifty of its buddies to turn up, then charges at you?

Answers on page 74

SNAKES

How, I hear you say, have we got so far through a book about jungles without even mentioning snakes? Surely they're slithering everywhere. Venomous ones ready to sink their fangs into you at the slightest provocation, or gigantic anacondas trying to crush the life out of you.

The answer is... "BECAUSE IT'S NOT LIKE THAT!"

All that stuff is just what you see in Hollywood films to make you think jungles are really scary and dangerous places. Snakes are sweet — well, maybe that's going a little bit too far — but the point is, virtually every snake you come across in the rainforest is going to be more scared of you than you are of it.
Most are harmless, and even the poisonous ones will sense the vibrations you make as you clomp along the ground and slither away to hide long before you turn up.
You hardly ever see them. Honestly!
Having said that, there are several to watch out for...

PUBLIC WARNING

Desperadoes on the Loose — The Snake Gang.

Fer de lance

Deadly poisonous. Do not approach as may bite even if not provoked. Once bitten, your flesh swells up and you bleed out of your pores. Sometimes your swollen flesh bursts open then falls off in strips (thankfully you would be dead before you saw this happen).

Coral Snake

Deadly dangerous, but they have small jaws with the fangs at the back which means they have little chance of opening their mouths wide enough to get a good bite.

Not to be confused with the False Coral Snake (left), the snake impressionist that just wants to look tough so no one else attacks it.

If you do get bitten by a poisonous snake, pray that it has given you a "dry bite," that is, not injected much venom. Remember, you are far too big for them to eat and snakes spend weeks building up their poison reserves. They don't want to go wasting it on some blundering explorer who doesn't watch where they are going.

Knowing whether the snake that has just bitten you is deadly or not is an important skill all explorers should know. If bitten by a brightly colored coral snake, make sure you notice the order in which the colored bands on the snake appear.

Just remember . . .

"Yellow, red, black – all right jack"
"Black, yellow, red – you're dead"

Hum it as you go along.

72

Anacondas

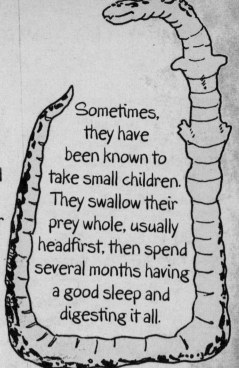

They can be huge — ten meters or so — but they are not poisonous. They tend to live in rivers and swamps, and use their huge weight to pull their prey under the water where they drown them.

Sometimes, they have been known to take small children. They swallow their prey whole, usually headfirst, then spend several months having a good sleep and digesting it all.

You're starting to feel like you're traveling from nowhere to nowhere. When you wake up in the morning, you are surrounded by leaves, branches and tree trunks, and each time you make camp, you get the same again. You plough forward, marking your way, machete cutting through vine tangles without any real idea now of where you are. At least your backpack is getting lighter as you eat your way through your food supplies. But what will happen when they run out? You haven't brought a gun to hunt for food and none of the streams you cross contain any fish that you might try to catch. If you don't find the Namweyos Indians soon, you may have to consider giving up this whole Lost City idea and heading back to the river where you can catch some fish to eat.

AGGRAVATED ANIMALS — ANSWERS

1. C

Giant Anteaters are very
short-sighted although
they are very aggressive
creatures. If you stay still
and keep your distance,
you should be fine.

GIANT
ANTEATER

2. E

White-lipped peccaries are probably the
most dangerous large animals in the
Amazon. They travel in herds of up to a
hundred. The clacking of their tusks as
they snuffle through the leaves for roots
and grubs can be heard a long way
away. They also smell pretty
awful — something like stale
sweat. When annoyed, they
charge. The only way to escape
is to climb up a tree. Even then,
peccaries have been known to
crowd around at the bottom
and try to uproot the tree!

WHITE-LIPPED
PECCARIES

3. D

Once buried in their hole, the armadillos are protected by
their huge shell. This works well against all predators,
except for people with guns. Sadly,
giant armadillos are becoming very
rare these days.

GIANT ARMADILLO

4. B

Sloths are so slow-moving that people (and presumably most predators) never notice them. Their hairs are grooved and hold green algae (like pond scum), which camouflages them against the forest foliage. If you see a sloth on the ground, it has usually come down to go to the toilet, something they only do about once a week. Sloths never poop from up in the trees, probably because they hang upside down all day.

5. A

Springing up into the air and running away quickly is meant to startle predators into thinking "what the heck was that?" They remain so stunned, they forget to attack, or so the armadillo hopes.

LONG-NOSED ARMADILLO

On walking through the forest, you find this...

FRESH CUTS

OOZING SAP

What does it mean?

A. You've walked in a circle. These are your own trail markings from two days ago.

B. This is someone else's trail. The Namweyos? It might be worth following to see where it leads.

C. This is just a tapir trail. Ignore it and carry on.

Read on and find out whether you are right.

Chapter 6
THE VILLAGE

Day 10: Food supplies: running low. Out of sugar and chocolate. Some rice left — not enough to last.

So, answer B was right.

THIS IS A trail and it's not yours. You can be sure of that because the marks are lower than you would cut (maybe whoever cut them was smaller than you), and there are footprints... bare human footprints!

It's much faster walking on a path than just blundering through the rainforest like you've been doing for the last few days. Animals realize this too. You'll see jaguar, puma, and tapir tracks in the mud that you are treading in. Insects also fly along these open areas — and spiders, realizing this, hang their webs at head height (because this is where most insects must fly) and try to stop them.

One of the most unpleasant things about walking along a jungle trail is getting a mouthful of spider. One second you're racing along, thrilled at walking so fast after all that jungle hacking, the next, you've got a sticky web stretched across your face and an enormous spider sitting on your nose. You have to flick it off quickly, before it bites you. Then you can spit the dead flies from the web out of your mouth.

WHAT ARE INDIANS REALLY LIKE?
Your questions answered

1. WHAT DOES AN INDIAN LOOK LIKE?

A. The Comanche witch doctor look?

B. Bowler hat and big, wide dress?

C. Casual streetwise?

D. Not many clothes, bowl haircut, and blowpipe?

2. WHAT DO THEY EAT?

A. Manioc, plantains and other crops?

B. Peccaries and other wild meat?

C. Turtle eggs?

D. River fish?

3. HOW DO THEY HUNT FOR THEIR FOOD?

A. With a bow and arrow?

B. Using a blowpipe and poisoned darts?

C. With a gun?

D. With a spear?

4. HOW DO THEY TRAVEL AROUND?

A. On foot?
B. By dugout canoe?
C. By bicycle?
D. By truck?

5. HOW WILL THEY REACT WHEN THEY SEE ME?

A. Shoot me full of arrows?
B. Run and hide in the forest?
C. Want all my high tech gear and maybe my money too?
D. Worship me as a god?

Now see if you had the right idea...

1. **Appearance**
Any one of these, except that A is a North American Indian and B is a highland Aymara Indian from the Andes Mountains.

2. **Diet**
All of these — anything edible they can get hold of — jungle animals, river fish, turtle eggs. The Yanomani of Venezula especially like fried tarantula legs! Not all the items in the Indians' diet may sound that appealing, but when the only source of food is the forest around you, you have to adapt. And if you think, tarantulas' legs or toadstools sound pretty yucky, think: we are happy to eat ground-up cows mixed with fat and breadcrumbs — just go into any burger restaurant.

3. Hunting

All of these things might be used. Some Indian tribes, like the Xavantes of Brazil, are renowned for their prowess with the bow. Some are taught how to shoot the bow with their feet. This lets you really pull the bow back and get a lot of power into the shot.

XAVANTE INDIAN

POINTED BAMBOO
(general use)

BLUNT
(for birds)

TRIPLE HOOK
(for fish)

Arrows have special heads for different targets like fish, birds or game. Sometimes the Indians use poisoned arrowheads. For instance, when hunting monkeys, a muscle relaxant called curare that is taken from a certain type of vine is used. Curare relaxes the monkey's muscles so much that they go all floppy and it falls to the ground from the trees.

Curare is also sometimes used in human surgery as a muscle relaxant.

LOOSE, FLOPPY SPIDER MONKEY

Some tribes use poison from the skin of very colorful tree frogs. These are colored in reds, yellows, or even blue to warn predators against eating them. They are deadly. Their poison can even go through your skin.

EXTRACT OF BOILED FROG

POISON ARROW FROG **Never touch a frog in the jungle!**

Blowpipes are only used by a few tribes in the Amazon, like the Waorani in Ecuador. The darts are poisoned and used for hunting birds. These days, many people use shotguns, as they are far more deadly and easier to use than bows or blowpipes.

4. Transportation

The answer depends on what sort of area the Indians live in and whether there are good roads. In some places, where the ground is more open and there are good tracks, some Indians have bikes, horses, or even cars. It is important to realize that many of the people living in the Amazon basin are Indian or part Indian. There are still a few who live what we would call "traditional" lives, but there are many more who live more or less like you and me.

5. Reaction

Any of these, except D. The Namweyos might just ignore you. You might not be interesting enough to be worth stopping their day to day business for. No matter how "untouched" you think they are, they most likely know all about "civilization" and have probably seen lots of people like you already.

THE NAMWEYOS
"MALOCA"

The Maloca

The people here are eager to show you their maloca, or communal house. You'll be surrounded by children who show you everything, like some of the men who aren't hunting, lazing in their hammocks, and several women who are chewing up manioc and spitting it back into the pot they got it from. This is to make cassiri — an alcoholic drink made from fermented manioc.

INSIDE THE HOUSE

By the way, the manioc is poisonous!
Raw manioc contains cyanide. So, how did
people discover you had to cook it?

Inside the maloca, it is dark and smokey. There are sleeping places for around thirty people, with hammocks slung in family groups. There aren't many possessions lying around. Nobody owns much. Most things are shared – including your stuff if you are not careful. People may look through your equipment and borrow things. This isn't necessarily stealing. They just might not have the same idea that the antique watch handed down to you by your grandparents really is so vitally important to you. Remember though you don't want to lose your equipment, you don't you want to lose the help of the Namweyos. They are the only people that know the trails to the mountains.

And before they do that, they may want to consult their chief or their medicine man ...

Medicine Man

Many Amazonian tribes don't have one person who is the leader or, if they do, their chief isn't all-powerful like some of our leaders like to think they are. Some tribes have medicine men or "shaman" who have special knowledge of the plants of the forest and know how to extract medicinal drugs from them. Some can put themselves into trances supposedly to talk with the spirits of the animals of the forest, or to see through the eyes, and communicate with, members of their tribe many miles away. Whether or not you believe in their powers is up to you, but many people have become convinced, especially when they have been told about things that the medicine man couldn't possibly have known about.

In 1997, a young Norwegian man named Lars, who was working at a Tacana Indian village in the Bolivian rainforest, set off in search of a remote tribe that might be able to help him with his studies of medicinal plants. He became lost and when he came to a large river, he decided that the best thing to do was to build a balsa wood raft and float downstream until he met someone who could help him get back to his village. When he finally returned to his village after seven weeks away, the villagers said he looked like a skinny howler monkey, as he had lost so much weight and grown a bushy red beard.

But, they said, they hadn't been too worried about him. They had known where he was the whole time. Francisco Navi had told them.

Francisco Navi was the village medicine man. Lars said he had an almost electric power you could feel when you shook his hand. Francisco Navi told Lars all about his trip.

"Remember when you were starving and you looked under that bush and found those jungle potatoes?"

Lars remembered.

"I put them there," the shaman said.

Every time Lars had needed help, Navi said, he had been there with him.

HOW TO SHRINK A HEAD

The Shuar of the upper Amazon in Ecuador used to be headhunters. They would raid the villages of nearby tribes, stealing the women and children, killing the men and cutting off their heads. For a Shuar to become a "man," he had to have taken at least one head in battle. They believed that if they kept the heads, they would retain the power of the warrior they had killed. This is how they preserved them.

INSTRUCTIONS (For reading only!)

1. Take one freshly-severed human head and slit down the back.
2. Peel back the skin and squeeze out the skull.
3. Sew the eyes, and the nostrils closed and the gap where you took the skull out, but leave an opening where the neck would join.
4. Heat up some sand and pour it in the head, along with various herbs.
5. Repeat several times using hot and then cold sand.

The result . . .
one shrunken head!

Now, you have a problem. The Namweyos are friendly enough to you. They keep you fed while you stay in their village, but they have no idea why you are here. They don't understand a word you say and you don't understand them. You've tried to explain in sign language that you want to go to the mountains. You've drawn pictures in the sand of temples in the jungle. But all that's happened is that you've been given more manioc to eat than you thought was possible to fit in and had the medicine man talk to you for hours on end (you didn't have a clue what he was saying).

After four days of hanging around, by which time you are on the point of giving up your expedition and leaving, two teenage boys whose names are Tico and Tubachi pick up your backpack and walk to the edge of the clearing. Then, without any words of farewell to their tribe, they set off into the rainforest. You follow them. You have no choice. They have your stuff!

TICO

TUBACHI

Chapter 7

INTO THE MOUNTAINS

Day 14: Food supplies: Enough for four days — some boiled manioc and strips of tapir meat the Namweyos have given you. 1 bag of rice — emergency reserve.

TICO AND TUBACHI, your Namweyos guides move quickly. They weave between the undergrowth plants almost silently as you slosh though the mud as fast as you can, bumping into palm trees and constantly losing the way. Each time you leave the trail, Tico whistles at you and nods in the direction you should be going.

Tubachi grins and says something of which you only catch the last part as he flicks his eyes toward you and giggles. Then you are off again, slipping, getting tangled in vines, and lagging farther and farther behind.

At one point, you see your guides ahead. They are crouching, perfectly still. You wheeze your way up to them just in time to see a long spotted tail disappearing into the undergrowth. You think you can make out a cat-like body — it has spots on its neck, blotchy circles on its side — then it is gone. . . .

"*Tigre*," your guides whisper. But it's not a tiger — they live in Asia — so what kind of large cat is it?

It could be a margay, an ocelot, or a jaguar. . . .

Margay – Stripy neck, spots, long tail
Ocelot – Stripes on neck, spots, short tail
Jaguar – Large, but can vary in size. Spots clustered into "rosettes"

Sometimes you get black jaguars, just as there are black panthers in Asia. If you were to look carefully, you would still see their spots, but they are mottled over a dark background coat. Black jaguars are rare, and in many places, local people think they are magic, a sign of very bad — or good luck. By the way, did you remember that jaguars kill their prey by biting through the skull? Something to think about when your head is sticking out of your sleeping shelter on those dark jungle nights.

Did you get it? The cat was a margay — the mixture of spots and stripes, and the long tail, should have given it away!

It's hard to tell margays and ocelots apart. Margays are usually smaller — less than one meter. They hunt animals in the trees and have ankles that can swivel around, so they can climb down tree trunks. Ocelots hunt on the ground and their bodies are longer and lower for pushing through undergrowth.

You're rising up towards the mountains now and the jungle feels different. It's cooler and, if anything, even wetter. There are tree ferns, and many of the trees are covered with moss and decked with spiky clusters of leaves called bromeliads. You have arrived in the cloud forest! Up on these slopes is where clouds condense every night. The plants get their water directly from them.

BROMELIAD

The bromeliads live on the branches, hitching a lift to get to the sunlight. They gather water in the "cup" beneath their leaves. This is useful to know if you want a drink but watch out for insects, mosquito larvae, and even tadpoles that make their home in these high-rise pools.

TREE FERN AND
BROMELIADS

Your guides do not know this forest very well. They only come occasionally here to hunt some of the colorful birds for their feathers, and to gather cinchona bark which they use as a medicine against malaria.

COCK-OF-THE-ROCK

There is one creature they are very scared of up here, but they have never seen it... THE MONKEY KING. This is how they describe it...

- As big as a man
- Brown or black with long shaggy fur
- It lives on the high ridges, on the soft pulp heart in the middle of a type of palm tree
- It rips the palms up with its bare hands and is so strong, it can throw a man as if he were a stick
- It can swing in the trees like a spider monkey
- It looks like a spider monkey, but has no tail
- It has a dog-like face with white marks on it

So...
What can it be?

Maybe a spectacled bear... a giant ape... or a tailless spider monkey?

SPECTACLED BEAR

There are plenty of rumors about these mysterious creatures in the South American jungle, but no one has ever caught one. The only evidence is a single photograph of a dead one taken by a group of explorers in Venezuela in 1920, who shot an ape-like creature when it attacked them. But the explorers were out of food and being shot at with arrows from time-to-time by hostile Indians. Afterwards, their leader said, "The body did not suffer the hardships of the journey." The skull, which they had used to keep their salt in, collapsed. The skin presumably went rotten, but what happened to the rest? Rumor has it that the explorers were so hungry that they probably ate it.

THE "APE" SHOT BY
De LOYS IN 1920

The route you are taking now is up one of the knife-edge ridges that lead up into the mountains. There is no obvious trail to follow and Tico and Tubachi pick their way through the dripping vegetation rather than cut it away with a machete. From time-to-time, you have to cross slippery mudslides where the ground has fallen away. Your barefoot guides scamper across easily, but more than once you slip and are only stopped from falling when one of their hands shoots out of the misty forest and pulls you back to safety. Suddenly, near to the ridge top, Tubachi stops. There seems no reason for this at all until you notice the rocks that the roots of the trees are growing up from. They are square-edged and equal-sized. They are bricks. This was once a wall. Tico and Tubachi will go no further, but they don't mind you continuing. They start gathering palm fronds to make a roof for a shelter and point at you to go forward....

Chapter 8

HOW LOST IS A LOST CITY?

Day 16: Food supplies: Low and getting moldy (still got the rice reserve).

FACT
There are lost cities in the South American jungle. People are still finding them. But how do they stay lost? And if they are truly lost, how come no one has ever found them before?

Well . . . we're in a rainforest here. Everything grows at such an alarming rate that anything that isn't growing, rots down rapidly.

Fungus and mold turn any wood or cloth to mush in a matter of months. Iron rusts. Copper disintegrates. Stone remains, but even that gets broken apart by roots that squeeze into the cracks, prying it apart and making walls crumble and topple. Leaves fall and rubble becomes soil. Soon, trees and ferns grow over everything. Give it a hundred years and your clearing — or lost city — looks much the same as the surrounding forest. You could be standing in the remains of a city and never know it.

It doesn't take long for the first vines and creepers to grow into any gap in the rainforest, for instance, where a large tree has fallen down. Tree weeds, like balsa and cecropia, whose seeds are blown in the wind, come in next.

They shoot up rapidly to form a canopy of parasol leaves to soak up as much sunlight as possible. Over the years, other trees grow up from underneath, ones whose seeds have been brought in the droppings of animals, like tapirs or fruit-eating birds, like orependolas. Some seeds are even planted carefully by animals

AGOUTI

like agoutis. These creatures bury brazil nuts for safe-keeping, but often forget where they have hidden them.

Lost cities are lost because they look so much like the surrounding forest that no one has spotted them yet. If they are still standing, then someone will have found it — some Indian farmer or hunter will know about the place, or maybe it's a sacred or forbidden place for the tribe.

The American archaeologist-explorer Hiram Bingham "discovered" the Inca citadel of Machu Picchu in 1911. He traveled through the cloud-forested mountains of Peru, searching for the lost city that the Incas had retreated to after Spanish Conquistadors invaded their capital, Cuzco. Hiram had to cross rickety suspension bridges over raging rivers, hack through bamboo thickets, and clamber up spindly, wooden ladders up cliff faces. But he wouldn't have found the now world-famous ruins had it not

been for an Indian farmer who turned up at his camp. The man said there were some remains of houses close to the top of a nearby mountain, and that he could lead Hiram there — for a price! Next morning, in the drizzly rain, they headed up the mountain, clambering 700 meters up through snake-infested long grass and gripping onto rock faces with the tips of their fingers.

But when Hiram reached the top, there were people there already — a group of smiling indians welcomed the explorers with gourds of cool, delicious water.

Hiram Bingham later found another city further into the rainforest.
He called this *Espiritu Pampa* — "the plain of ghosts." Because it was so covered in growth, he never realized how big it was. He was later to discover that *Espiritu Pampa*, not Machu Picchu, was the true lost capital of the Incas.

More recently, also in Peru, remains of another lost civilization were discovered. The Chachapoyas lived at the same time as the Incas (about 600 years ago), and it seems they battled with them — hundreds of axe and spear heads were found. Some ruins were also uncovered as were graves of mummified bodies. Unfortunately, many of the tombs had been robbed and destroyed as looters made off with any gold and precious stones they could find. A lost city doesn't stay lost for long.

But sometimes ruins do get discovered just by chance. Until 1995, no one knew of the huge Mayan temple pyramids at Tulum in Guatemala, Central America. They were so grown over that people thought they were just hills. It was only when a satellite photo was taken from space that archaeologists realized that these hills were too evenly spaced to be natural. They traveled to the area and dug away at the undergrowth and soil that had built up, until they found the remains of some temples, but the big discovery was made entirely by chance. One day, one of the archaeologists was exploring around the edge of the ruins when he fell down a pit. He caught himself just in time — his top half was just above the ground while his legs dangled above what he thought must be a den of poisonous snakes. For hours, he didn't move or make a sound, terrified of being bitten. Finally, one of his companions found him and pulled him out. The pit wasn't full of snakes. It was deep — three stories deep in fact! They had been standing on the top floor of a huge temple and never even realized!

All these stories were about cities of stone, so there was still something to find. But in many places in the Amazon, there wasn't enough stone to build with. Before the Europeans arrived, hundreds of thousands of people lived along the Amazon. In the plains of Bolivia, which flood for half of the year, lived a great civilization known as the Moxos. They built their cities on huge mounds of earth and drained the swampy land with canals. Their settlements were made of wood with woven palm-thatch roofs. Today, the dikes and mounds built by the Moxos remain. The cities do not.

Look at the picture. This is what you find when you go on beyond the outer wall that Tico and Tubachi would not pass. Can you make out where the temple pyramid is? Look at the clues.

Can you figure out what animal has made its lair in the rubble at the bottom?

When you shine a flashlight into the opening, a pair of eyes reflect back orange at you, then blink out as their owner turns its head away. You catch a glimpse of its coat – dark splodgy rings on a lighter background.

By now, you should realize what the animal is, especially now as it starts to growl a low, revving trundling, like a rusty old truck being started up. Still not got it? The clues...cat-like tracks... turns its head away from the flashlight...rosette spot pattern and rumbling growl....

JAGUAR!

And it's running out towards you!

You stand frozen for a second. Half in terror, half in the crazed idea that you might be able to face it off.

The jaguar leaps...

...right over you...landing almost silently on the ground behind you and disappearing instantly into the foliage.

You are shaken. Your heart is beating fast, but you edge forward to investigate an object in the cave which is glistening in the glow of your flashlight-beam. It's a gold figurine — half-man and half-cat — some god or demon. It's the proof you need to show to a doubting world that after so many hardships, you have actually found the lost city you set out to discover.

When you get home, you'll be famous. TV, newspapers, the whole world's press will want to know how you did it... when you get home!

But you have to get home first. Can you work out the way? Here's a map. Work out which hexagons you will have to go through to retrace your route.

WARNING:
You have not visited all of the places on the map.

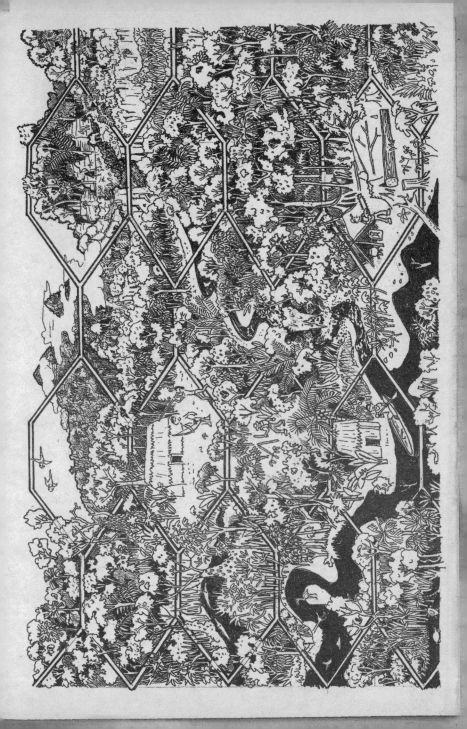

ANSWER

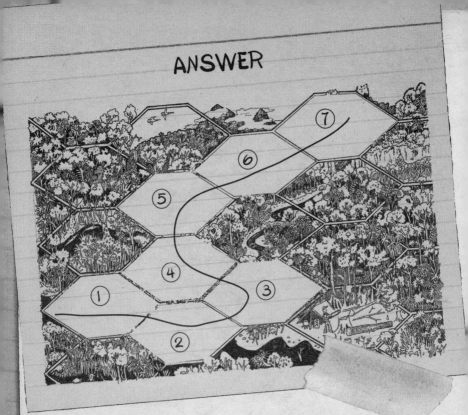

Of course, to return, you'll still need the skills you have learned during your journey to the lost city. Tico and Tubachi can take you back to their village, but from there you'll be on your own again. You'll have to find the trail you made from the waterfall and hope you marked your way well enough to follow it back without getting lost.

If your canoe is still where you sunk it in the river, you can paddle that downstream. If it's not there, you'll have to find some dry balsa logs and build a raft. Whichever way you travel on the river, you'll have to watch out for the rapids and control your craft well. If you capsize, you could lose everything. If you make it through, Manolo and his family should be pleased to see you.

Manolo might even
help you paddle the canoe
for the rest of your trip back —
you could treat him to
some new clothes and give him
the canoe — you won't need it anymore.

It's time to head home until your next adventure. You've proved yourself IN THE JUNGLE, but what next? New challenges await you: *Under the Sea, On Safari, In the Wilderness, On the South Sea Islands, In the Himalayas, In the Desert,* and *At the North Pole.*

EXPLORERS WANTED!

Your mission...

should you choose to accept it,
is to head up a diving expedition in search
of sunken treasure and the SS *Desdemona*.

Are you ready for the challenge?

Explorers Wanted to:

- Learn how to dive
- Navigate coral reefs
- Brave extreme conditions
- Encounter strange sea life
- Descend to the deepest depths

Includes the author's own expedition notes and sketches!

EXPLORERS
WANTED!
UNDER THE SEA

Simon Chapman

SO ... YOU WANT TO BE AN UNDERWATER EXPLORER?

Do you want to ...
Dive among the coral reefs ...?

Search for **treasure** in **sunken wrecks** ...?

Descend to the bottom of the **deepest** ocean trench?

If the answer to any of these questions is **YES**,

then this is the book for you. Read on ...

107

THIS BOOK WILL tell you how to get started — from exploring with a snorkel or diving with a tank of air on your back, to discovering the secrets of the deepest depths in a mini-submarine. There are also some pretty scary true-life stories of some of the people who have tried to explore it before ... so read on!

YOUR MISSION ...

should you choose to accept it, is to lead a diving expedition — in search of sunken treasure.

You'll be diving around the reef-fringed South Seas island of Motorua, looking for the wreck of the SS Desdemona that sank in a storm in 1909 (see expedition dossier at the end of this chapter). The island lies along a geological faul line and its coral reefs plunge down a steep rift wall far deeper than anyone can dive without some really special equipment. To explore the reef, the wall and its depths, you are going to need training.

Is the SS *Desdemona* going to be impossible to find?

What kind of treasure are you trying to find in her watery grave?

IT'S UP TO YOU TO FIND OUT.

You are going to need to learn about what you might find in the ocean, and how to survive where there is no air to breathe and thousands of tons of water pressure pushing on you.

Time to set the scene ...

Let's find out some vital facts about the ocean and its environment before the mission gets under way.

Seventy-one percent of the Earth's surface is covered with water. What you find, whether it's open ocean, coral reefs, kelp forests, or deep ocean trenches, depends on where you go ... and how deep.

Coral reefs are the tropical rainforests of the sea. This maps shows where in the world to find them.

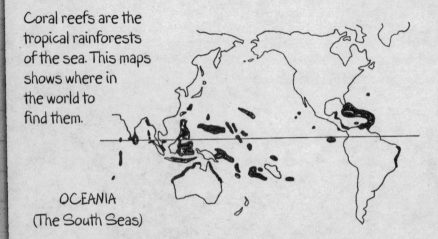

OCEANIA
(The South Seas)

Another thing you might notice under the sea is that the water gets darker as you descend deeper. Sunlight is absorbed by any particles floating around. They take out the red and yellow colors in sunlight, allowing bluer colors to get through (sunlight is made up of all the colors of the rainbow). That's why sea water looks bluish. In the deepest parts of the ocean depths, no light gets through at all. It is pitch black. Lots of the animals that live down there have luminous markings, so that they can find others of their own kind or hunt for food.

So, what's the sea really like under the surface?
Put your head underwater and have a look.

It's wet (obviously), cold (unless, that is, you've started off
somewhere tropical), you can't breathe (also obvious), and it's
all blurry....

Not being able to see properly is one thing that you can do
something about right away. Your eyes aren't designed to
work underwater, so it helps if you wear a pair of goggles.

There are a few more things to see now...

Wearing a good pair of goggles will make things look slightly nearer (and so bigger), than they really are ... how big was that fish you saw? As for feeling cold and not being able to breathe, these are two things that can be avoided if you wear the right equipment. But the biggest problem you will face will be ...

THE PRESSURE!

This doesn't mean it's going to be hard and stressful to understand all this stuff. It's just that when you dive under, you will have a huge amount of water pushing on top of you — one liter of water weighs one kilogram. Think how much weight of water you will have above you just a few meters down. Heavy, eh?

Now here comes the science!

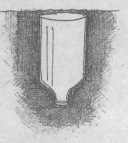

When you are underwater, pressure pushes equally from all directions. This pressure increases the deeper down you go.

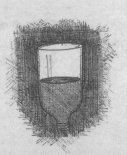

At ten meters down, there's twice the pressure there was at the surface. The air in this bottle would squash to half its size.

At 90 meters down, there's ten times the pressure. The air in the bottle would now take up a tenth of the space.

The water pressure hundreds of meters down in the ocean would crush you. What's more, going up quickly to the surface later can be a huge problem too. Gases in your blood expand as the pressure on them lessens, which can be very nasty. Many deep-sea fish puff out and burst when they are brought to the surface because of this! So would you if you held your breath at the seabed then rapidly rose to the surface.

BEFORE   AFTER

Face it, just to survive at all, let alone explore, you are going to have to overcome these difficulties...

· How to breathe
· How to see
· How to stay warm
· How to cope with all that pressure, man!

The Wreck of the SS *Desdemona*
EXPEDITION DOSSIER

In 1909, the luxury liner, SS *Desdemona*, went down in a storm off the South Seas island of Motorua. Despite happening so far away from America, the sinking was widely reported in the papers at the time, mainly because of the loss of the "Fortune Star," a beautifully-cut diamond the size of an egg, which had been the

FORTUNE STAR

engagement present of Eva Meringue, the gorgeous actress fiancée of the millionaire industrialist, Jerry Steinburger. The couple had been about to get married aboard the ship when the storm had struck. They were lucky. Their cabin had been just below the level of the main deck, and they had been among the first to get away on one of the liner's few lifeboats.

EVA AND JERRY

But — sadly without the diamond! That had been left in the safe of their stateroom, and so it had sunk to the seabed, along with the SS *Desdemona* and most of the other passengers. As for the marriage — it never took place. "No gem, no wife," Eva told Jerry after a passing cargo ship picked up their lifeboat. She went on to a glittering career in the movies. He kept his millions and lived the rest of his life as a virtual recluse.

The story so far . . .
Everybody knows that divers have long searched the coral reefs of Motorua and, though they have found the wrecks of several other ships which storms have smashed to pieces on the reef, they have never located the SS *Desdemona*.

BUT NOW YOU HAVE AN IDEA!

Just recently, this life preserver from
the SS *Desdemona* was washed up
on the southern shore of the island.

WHAT IF... everybody has been
looking in the **wrong place?**

WHAT IF... strong currents pulling along the
undersea chasm, which runs along the
east side of the island, have dragged the wreckage
south — not north — as everyone had presumed?

This is the idea you recently presented to the Jerry Steinburger
foundation, who have given you funding for an expedition to
Motorua, and promised to reward you handsomely if you can
retrieve the diamond.

Just one small problem though...

You don't actually know how to dive!

It is obvious that you will
need training. Here's how
we'll do it. We'll have to start at
the top and get deeper... and
deeper.

About the author

Writer and broadcaster, Simon Chapman, is a self-confessed jungle addict, making expeditions whenever he can. His travels have taken him to tropical forests all over the world, from Borneo and Irian Jaya to the Amazon.

The story of his search for a mythical Giant Ape in the Bolivian rainforest, *The Monster of the Madidi*, was published in 2001. He has also had numerous articles and illustrations published in magazines in Britain, and the United States, including *Wanderlust*, *BBC Wildlife*, and *South American Explorer*, and has written and recorded for BBC Radio 4, and lectured on the organization of jungle expeditions at the Royal Geographical Society, of which he is a fellow. When not exploring, Simon lives with his wife and his two young children in Lancaster, England, where he teaches high school physics.